St. Luke
425 East 38th St.
Erie, PA 16504

THE HISTORY OF THE DETROIT LIONS

THE HISTORY OF THE
DETROIT

Published by Creative Education
123 South Broad Street
Mankato, Minnesota 56001
Creative Education is an imprint of The Creative Company.

DESIGN AND PRODUCTION BY **EVANSDAY DESIGN**

Copyright © 2005 Creative Education.
International copyright reserved in all countries.
No part of this book may be reproduced in any form
without written permission from the publisher.
Printed in the United States of America

LIBRARY OF CONGRESS CATALOGING-IN-PUBLICATION DATA

Frisch, Aaron.
The history of the Detroit Lions / by Aaron Frisch.
p. cm. — (NFL today)
Summary: Traces the history of the team from its beginnings through 2003.
ISBN 1-58341-296-4
1. Detroit Lions (Football team)—History—Juvenile literature.
[1. Detroit Lions (Football team)—History. 2. Football—History.]
I. Title. II. Series.

GV956.D4F75 2004
796.332'64'0977434—dc22   2003065038

First edition

9 8 7 6 5 4 3 2 1

COVER PHOTO: wide receiver Charles Rogers

LIONS

Aaron Frisch

THE CITY OF **DETROIT, MICHIGAN,** IS CONSIDERED THE CAR CAPITAL OF THE WORLD. IT WAS HERE THAT AUTOMOBILE PIONEER HENRY FORD BEGAN BUILDING THE FIRST CARS IN THE 1890S. TODAY THIS NORTHERN CITY IS HOME TO THE THREE AMERICAN CAR COMPANY GIANTS—FORD, GENERAL MOTORS, AND CHRYSLER—AND IS A MAJOR MANUFACTURER OF CAR PARTS AND OTHER STEEL PRODUCTS.

SINCE 1934, THE "MOTOR CITY" HAS ALSO BEEN KNOWN AS A FOOTBALL TOWN. THAT YEAR, A RADIO TYCOON AND FOOTBALL ENTHUSIAST NAMED GEORGE RICHARDS BOUGHT A STRUGGLING NATIONAL FOOTBALL LEAGUE (NFL) TEAM CALLED THE SPARTANS AND MOVED IT FROM PORTSMOUTH, OHIO, TO DETROIT. RENAMED THE LIONS (A NATURAL FIT ALONGSIDE THE CITY'S TIGERS BASEBALL TEAM), THE TEAM HAS BEEN ON THE PROWL EVER SINCE.

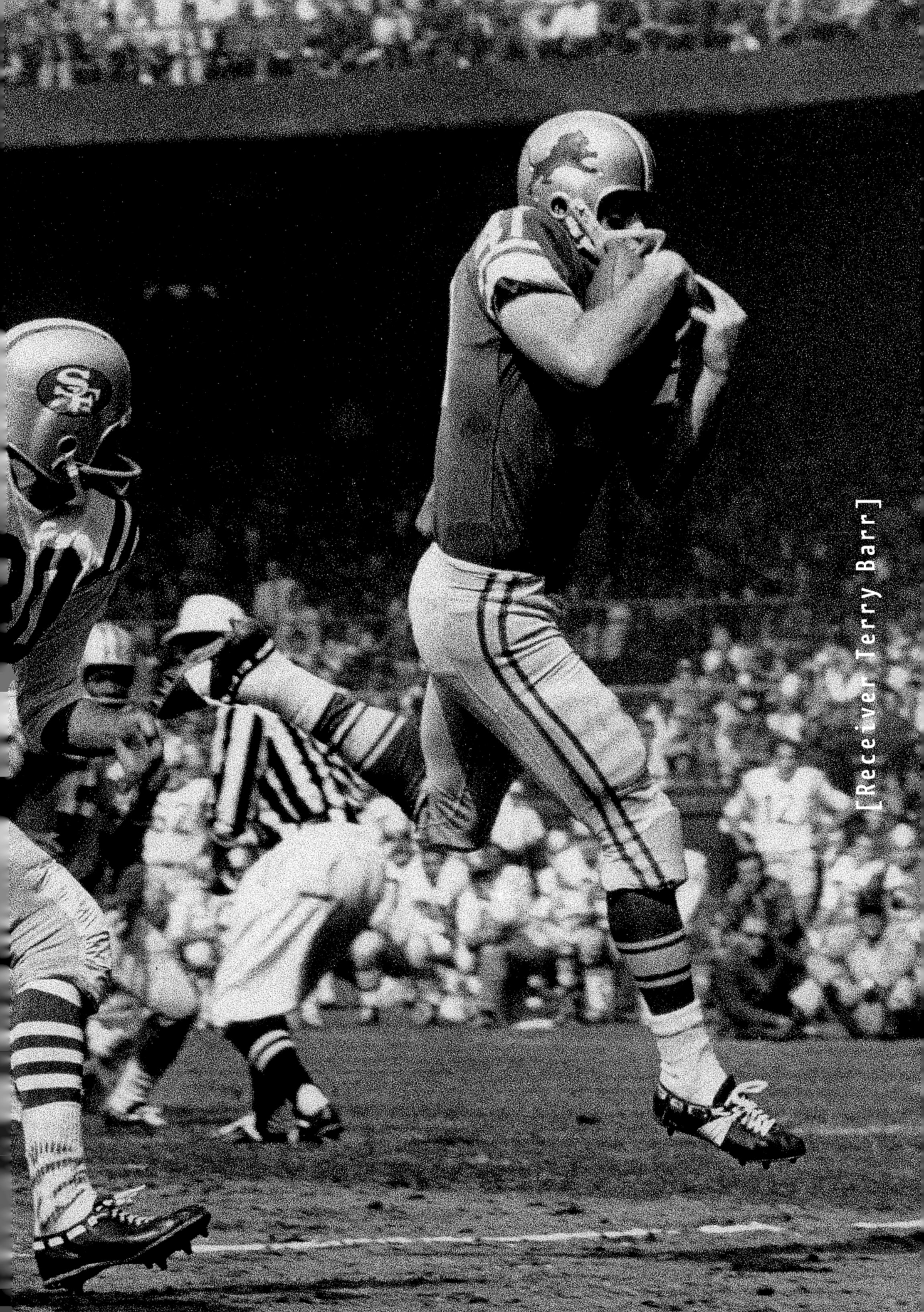
[Receiver Terry Barr]

A ROARING START>

WHEN THE LIONS settled in Detroit in 1934, the Tigers were a baseball powerhouse. But the Lions quickly got the attention of Michigan sports fans. The team had a ferocious defense featuring such stars as safety Glenn Presnell and linebacker Gover "Ox" Emerson. In their first season, the Lions went 10–3, not allowing a single point in their first seven games. They also made national headlines by playing in a special Thanksgiving Day game—a Lions tradition that continues to this day.

In 1935, Detroit charged all the way to the NFL championship game. As freezing rain turned the University of Detroit Stadium field into a muddy mess, the Lions mauled the New York Giants 26–7 to become league champions. One of the stars of that game was running back Earl "Dutch" Clark, the first great Lions rusher and a player renowned for his cool leadership. "If Dutch

The Lions delighted their fans by earning a reputation as a tough, brawling team right from the start.

Down! Cover 7 Set! Hut!

Cross 8! Cross 8! Set! Hut Hut!

stepped on the field with [football legends] Red Grange, Jim Thorpe, and George Gipp," an opposing coach once said, "Dutch would be the general."

The Lions remained a winning team the rest of the 1930s and continued to add talented players in the years that followed. Detroit had some of the NFL's brightest stars in the 1940s, including Alex Wojciechowicz, an undersized but fierce center and linebacker, and Bill Dudley, a versatile running back and kick returner nicknamed "Bullet Bill." Yet despite some great individual efforts, the '40s were a difficult decade for Detroit. In 1942, the Lions went an embarrassing 0–11. In 1946, 1947, and 1948, they finished in last place in the NFL's Western Division.

Things finally began looking up in the Motor City in 1950. That year, the team signed quarterback Bobby Layne and drafted a young running back named Doak Walker. With the help of Leon Hart—a huge, remarkable athlete who played both offensive and defensive end—the Lions went a respectable 6–6. In 1951, after former Lions running back Buddy Parker was named the team's head coach, Detroit jumped to 7–4–1. Suddenly, the Lions were back.

LAYNE LEADS TO GREATNESS>

THE 1950S WERE a glorious era in Detroit, and the player most responsible for those good times was Bobby Layne. Although his career statistics in passing yards and touchdowns were not overly impressive, Layne was a born leader whose toughness was unmatched. He became fiery when the situation called for it, but he preferred to inspire his teammates with his calm attitude, often cracking jokes in the huddle during the most tense situations. Layne hated defeat and refused to believe his team could be beaten. "Bobby never lost a game," Doak Walker once said. "The clock just ran out on him a couple of times, that's all."

In 1952, Layne, Walker, and Hart—along with star safety Jack Christiansen—led the Lions to a 9–3 record and the NFL championship game, where they faced the Cleveland Browns, one of the most consistently

Bobby Layne was a clutch performer who always seemed to play his best late in close games.

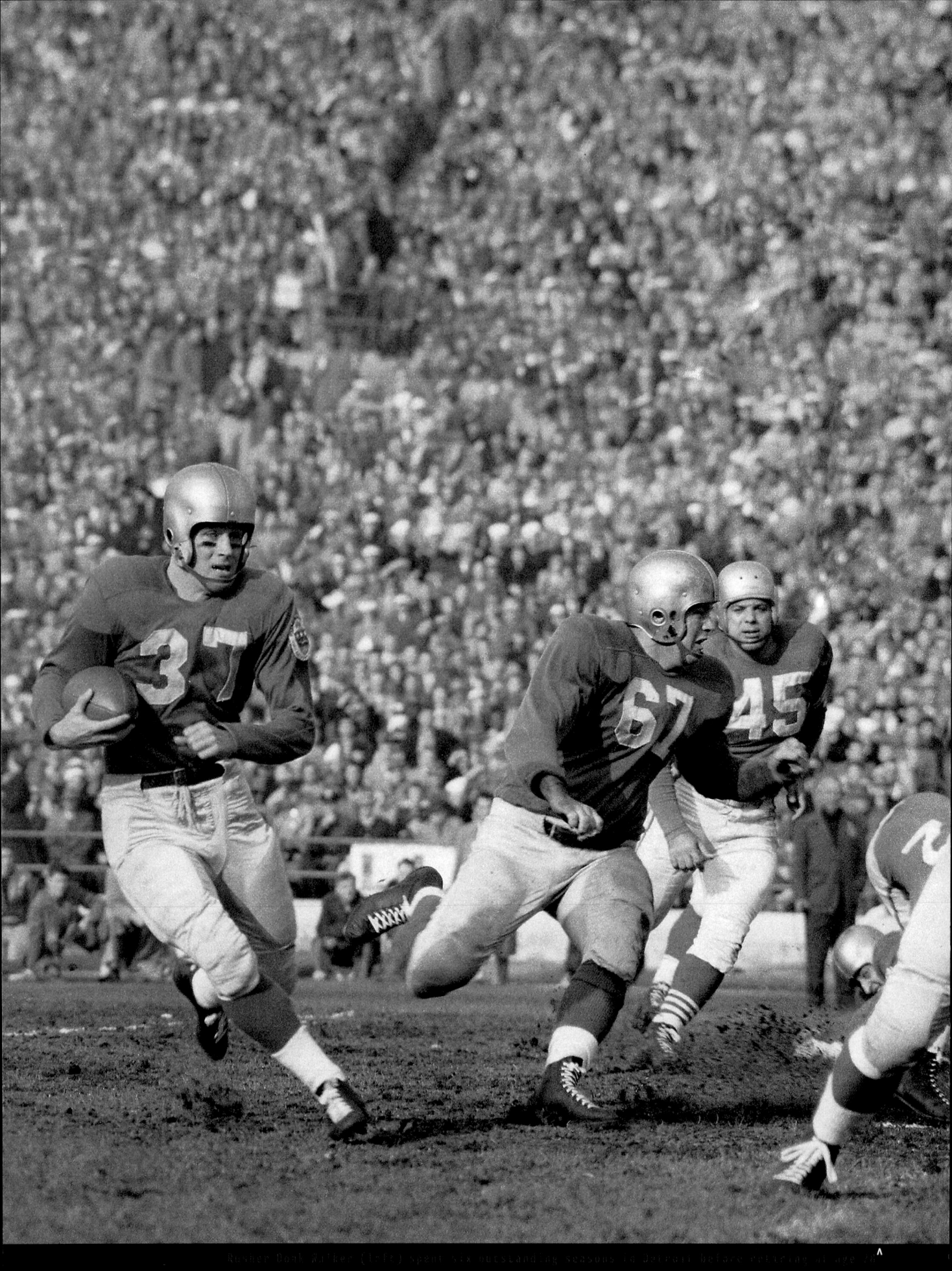

Rusher Doak Walker (left) spent six outstanding seasons in Detroit before retiring at age 28.

Cross 12 Cross 12! Set! Hut Hut!

powerful teams of the '50s. In the title game, Walker broke free for a 67-yard touchdown run as Detroit won 17–7 to capture its first NFL championship in 17 years.

The Lions faced the Browns again in the 1953 NFL championship game, a contest that added to Layne's legend. With four minutes left in the fourth quarter, Cleveland led 16–10. In the Lions' offensive huddle, Layne saw nervousness in his teammates' eyes. "Now if you'll just block a little bit, fellas," he said in his confident Texas drawl, "ol' Bobby'll pass you right to the championship." Eight plays later, he threw a 33-yard touchdown strike, and the Lions were NFL champs for the second year in a row.

Layne led his team to the championship game again in 1954, but the Lions finally lost the title to the Browns. In 1957, the star quarterback was injured during the season. His backup, Tobin Rote, came in and led the way as Detroit won its fourth NFL title, crushing Cleveland 59–14 in the championship game. A year later, Detroit fans said goodbye to the greatest leader in Lions history when Layne was traded away.

DOING IT WITH DEFENSE>

EVEN WITHOUT LAYNE, the Lions hardly skipped a beat, finishing second in the Western Division in 1960, 1961, and 1962. The Lions had a fierce defense during those years. Linebacker Joe Schmidt earned the nickname "Red Dog" for his aggressive playing style. Safety Yale Lary was one of the game's top ball hawks, making 50 interceptions during his Lions career. And cornerback Dick "Night Train" Lane earned a fearsome reputation as a headhunter for his habit of hitting opposing ball-carriers high and hard.

Another player who frightened opponents during those years was defensive tackle Alex Karras. At 270 pounds, Karras was as strong as an ox and capable of single-handedly collapsing offensive lines. But he was also incredibly fast and relentless in his pursuit. Offensive linemen could not match his speed; sometimes running backs couldn't either.

In addition to his defensive skills, Yale Lary (left) was the NFL's best punter in the early '60s.

"Running away from Karras is worse than running at him," said Baltimore Colts running back Lenny Moore. "He moves so fast on those stumpy legs, and you can hear him closing in on you from behind. I hate that sound. You get this feeling like you're about to be buried by a buffalo stampede."

The Detroit defense proved just how good it was in 1962 during a classic Thanksgiving Day game against the 10–0 Green Bay Packers. The Lions swarmed all over legendary Packers quarterback Bart Starr throughout the afternoon. Detroit led 23–0 at halftime and won 26–14 in what one sportswriter called "one of the most memorable displays of aggressive defensive football ever witnessed."

But as good as the Lions defense was, it was not good enough to bring Detroit another NFL title. Such players as receiver Terry Barr gave some great performances throughout the 1960s, but the team could never win the Western Division to earn another shot at a championship.

Linebacker Joe Schmidt was a longtime Lions captain famous for his "clean but mean" tackling style.

A fast, swarming defense has been a Lions trademark throughout most of the team's history

FROM THE '70s TO SIMS>

AS THE 1970S began, the Lions were eager to return to championship form. They featured a number of new standouts during that time, including center Ed Flanagan, cornerback Lem Barney, and tight end Charlie Sanders. Unfortunately, the '70s proved to be frustrating years. The Minnesota Vikings ruled the new National Football Conference (NFC) Central Division throughout the decade, and Detroit finished second to the Vikings nearly every season.

In 1979, the Lions stumbled to a 2–14 record. The good news was that the poor record gave Detroit the first pick in the 1980 NFL Draft. With it, the team selected speedy running back Billy Sims, who had won the Heisman Trophy in 1978 as the nation's best college football player. The Lions hoped that Sims would provide the offensive boost they so badly needed.

Speedy star Billy Sims became just the second Detroit player to rush for 1,000 yards in a season

Sims started his NFL career in fine style. In his first game, he caught a short pass, dodged a linebacker, and ran 60 yards for a touchdown to fuel a Detroit win. During the 1980 season, Sims set a team record with 1,303 rushing yards, scored 13 touchdowns, and was named Rookie of the Year. Behind his performance, Detroit went 9–7. "I must admit," said Lions head coach Monte Clark, "as much as I like to stress team effort, Billy has been the big difference."

Detroit continued to improve, making the playoffs in 1982 and 1983. In the 1983 playoffs against the San Francisco 49ers, Lions kicker Eddie Murray tried a 25-yard field goal attempt with five seconds left to win the game. He missed by inches, and the Lions lost 24–23. That would be the team's last playoff game for eight years.

The 1984 season was a disaster. The Lions lost several close games and went just 4–11–1, but worst of all, they lost Sims to a severe knee injury. He came back the next season but was never the same. As Sims's performance went downhill, the Lions went down with him. Running back James Jones and defensive end Michael Cofer did their best to keep the team competitive, but it wasn't enough. The Lions became one of the worst teams in football in the late '80s.

Versatile halfback James Jones (right) did his best to boost the Lions offense during the late 1980s

THE SANDERS SENSATION>

THE 1989 SEASON felt like 1980 all over again. With the third pick in that year's NFL Draft, the Lions found a new star. Like Billy Sims, he was a fast running back who wore number 20 on his jersey. His name was Barry Sanders, and he quickly proved that he was even better than Sims had been. As a rookie, he broke Sims's team record by rushing for 1,470 yards.

That was just the start of one of the most amazing careers in NFL history. In his first six seasons, Sanders rushed for 8,672 yards—an average of 1,445 yards per year. And he did it in electrifying style. Sanders stood only 5-foot-9, but a combination of great balance, vision, and strength enabled him to spin, juke, and cut like no other runner in the game. "Barry is so good that sometimes during a game, I catch myself watching as a fan and not an opponent," said Tampa Bay Buccaneers linebacker Hardy Nickerson. "He does things that leave even pros' mouths hanging open."

Barry Sanders was perhaps the most elusive rusher in NFL history, capable of scoring on any play.

Also starring in Detroit during the early '90s were tough linebacker Chris Spielman, swift kick returner Mel Gray, offensive tackle Lomas Brown, and receiver Herman Moore. Besides Sanders, Moore became perhaps the Lions' brightest star after joining the team in 1991. The 6-foot-4 receiver had been an outstanding high jumper on his college track team, and he became known in the NFL for his ability to outleap defenders for high passes. These players led Detroit to a 12–4 record in 1991 and a 10–6 mark in 1993, winning the NFC Central both years. Unfortunately, the Lions were quickly beaten in the playoffs each time.

The late '90s were years of great individual achievement in Detroit. In 1995, Moore earned a special place in football history by catching an NFL-record 123 passes. Then, in 1997, Sanders charged for 2,053 rushing yards, becoming only the third running back ever to top the prestigious 2,000-yard mark. But despite these superhuman efforts, Detroit still could not find playoff success.

A huge target with terrific hands, Herman Moore set a Lions receiving record with 62 career touchdowns

A NEW FIELD AND FUTURE>

THE LIONS WERE dealt a stunning blow in 1999 when Sanders announced his retirement. Although he was only 30 years old and needed just 1,457 yards to surpass former Chicago Bears great Walter Payton as the NFL's all-time rushing leader, he felt the timing was right. "I always told myself I would play this game as long as it was fun," he explained. "When it became a job for me, I decided it was time to move on."

As injuries had also slowed Moore, the Lions were forced to find some new stars. Over the next few seasons, Detroit fans cheered for such new heroes as receiver Germane Crowell, linebacker Stephen Boyd, running back James Stewart, and quarterback Joey Harrington. In 2002, these players and the rest of the Lions left the Pontiac Silverdome—the team's home since 1975—and moved into Ford Field, a beautiful new stadium in downtown Detroit.

James Stewart was a key part of Detroit's rebuilding effort in the first seasons of the 21st century

Aggressive linebacker Stephen Boyd was the team's leading tackler every year from 1997 to 2000.

Michigan native Steve Mariucci was named coach in 2003

Fans hoped Joey Harrington would become a Lions star

The Lions struggled in the first few seasons of the 21st century, going 2–14 in 2001, 3–13 in 2002, and 5–11 in 2003. But two key additions in 2003 promised to boost Detroit up the standings in the new NFC North Division. First the team hired a new coach: Steve Mariucci, who had previously built a winning record with the San Francisco 49ers. Then the Lions selected Charles Rogers, a tall and blazing fast receiver from nearby Michigan State University, in the NFL Draft.

With an all-time roster that includes such names as Clarke, Layne, and Sanders, the Detroit Lions have featured their share of NFL greats. Yet in the five decades since winning their fourth NFL championship in 1957, the Lions have won only one playoff game. Today's Lions, settled in Ford Field and hungry for respect, hope to soon pounce on a Super Bowl trophy and make the Motor City a city of champions once again.

INDEX

B
Barney, Lem 20
Barr, Terry 5, 16
Boyd, Stephen 28, 30
Brown, Lomas 26

C
Christiansen, Jack 10
Clark, Earl (Dutch) 6, 9, 31
Clark, Monte 22
Cofer, Michael 22
Crowell, Germane 28

D
division championships 26
Dudley, Bill 9

E
Emerson, Gover (Ox) 6

F
Flanagan, Ed 20
Ford Field 28, 31

G
Gray, Mel 26

H
Harrington, Joey 28, 31
Hart, Leon 9, 10

J
Jones, James 22, 22–23

K
Karras, Alex 14, 16

L
Lane, Dick 14
Lary, Yale 14, 15
Layne, Bobby 9, 10, 11, 13, 31
Lions name 4

M
Mariucci, Steve 31, 31
Moore, Herman 26, 26–27, 28
Murray, Eddie 22

N
NFL championship games 6, 10, 13
NFL championships 6, 10, 13, 31
NFL records 26

P
Parker, Buddy 9
Pontiac Silverdome 28
Portsmouth Spartans 4
Presnell, Glenn 6

R
Richards, George 4
Rogers, Charles 31
Rote, Tobin 13

S
Sanders, Barry 24, 25, 26, 28, 31
Sanders, Charlie 20
Schmidt, Joe 14, 16–17
Sims, Billy 20, 21, 22, 24
Spielman, Chris 26
Stewart, James 28, 29

T
team records 22, 24
Thanksgiving Day games 6, 16

W
Walker, Doak 9, 10, 12–13, 13
Wojciechowicz, Alex 8–9, 9